CONOR
McGREGOR
SINGLENESS OF PURPOSE

Art by Richard Davies.
Design by Alexander Svelnis.

Fonts used: Adobe Text Pro, 1689 GLC Garamond Pro, Europa, League Gothic, WICKED GRIT.

Thanks to Graeme McDonnell of SevereMMA, Anders Ericsson, Stephen Guise, and Brian Tracy.

Quotes on cover and all interior artwork by Conor McGregor. Photography credit and quote source attributions in appendix.

ISBN: 978-1-77136-666-3

singlenessofpurposebook@gmail.com

CONOR
McGREGOR
SINGLENESS OF PURPOSE

BY ALEXANDER SVELNIS

I'VE LOST MY MIND DOING THIS GAME.
LIKE VINCENT VAN GOGH.
HE DEDICATED HIS LIFE TO HIS ART
AND LOST HIS MIND IN THE PROCESS.
THAT'S HAPPENED TO ME.

BUT FUCK IT.

WHEN THAT GOLD BELT IS AROUND MY WAIST,
WHEN MY MOTHER HAS A BIG MANSION,
WHEN MY GIRLFRIEND HAS A DIFFERENT CAR FOR EVERY DAY OF THE WEEK,
WHEN MY KIDS' KIDS HAVE EVERYTHING THEY EVER WANT,
THEN IT WILL PAY. THEN I'M HAPPY I LOSY MY MIND, YEAH?

I'LL DIE
A CRAZY
OLD
MAN.

From the mural on Clanbrassil Street in Dublin that proclaims, "**We're not here to take part. We're here to take over,**" to the Reebok shirts reminding everyone that "**The double champ does what the fuck he wants.**" These days, the words of Conor McGregor can be found all over the world.

Rewind to August 16, 2013—

Before the dolly went crashing through the bus window.

Before the suit had the letters FUCK YOU stitched in for its pinstripes.

Before the apology to absolutely nobody.

Before the Diaz brothers' red-panty nights.

Before the money.

Before the fame.

Before the thirteen-second knockout of Jose Aldo.

Before the tattoo of a gorilla eating a heart was needled into his chest.

Before he truly became *Notorious.*

And just 24 hours before his second UFC fight— Conor was reading quotes from a book he brought with him for his American debut.

He read a quote by Anatole France:

To accomplish great things, we must not only act, but also dream—not only plan, but also believe.

He read one by Oprah:

Your true passion should feel like breathing; it's that natural.

And he read one by Robert Collier:

Constant repetition carries conviction.

Conor said that "Constant repetition carries conviction" is his favorite quote during an interview with Off the Ball, March 27, 2014

"Some good shit, isn't that?" Conor asked his coach after reading the last quote.

"We're gonna decorate the gym with these," his coach replied.

"That's what I'm saying. These books are full of them. When I read quotes ... **I take from them.** And just put my own thing to it. You know what I mean? Say it in my own way."

Quotes and conversation from RTÉ's *Notorious* Documentary, March 13, 2014

As much as anything else, it has been Conor's ability to absorb the wisdom of others that has transformed him into who he is today.

This book contains over 150 of Conor's most inspiring and instructional quotes. But unless we understand the distinction Conor makes between reading them and "taking from" them, they offer us nothing. It is not enough to pass over the words lightly. They must be dwelled on and contemplated. That is what Conor has done with the wisdom he's encountered, and the effect it's had on him shows itself every time he speaks.

Never mind motivating UFC fighters and raising that bar. [I want to motivate all] humans—people just on their own journey—that anything can be achieved, and it can be achieved like that. If you put your head down, if you work, if you believe in yourself and you speak with confidence, and whatever you wanna do you speak it loud with no fear. And no matter what people say, it happens. So, that's something that I can take with me, and being able to do that actually inspires and motivates me right back.

Conor McGregor after London Press Conference, SevereMMA, July 14, 2017

YOU'RE AGAINST YOURSELF.

———

*U*h *vai morrer.*

Conor McGregor growled these words into the face of Jose Aldo during their first official stare-down on March 20, 2015. The exchange took place in front of a Rio de Janeiro crowd that was chanting the same phrase at Conor. In Jose's native Portuguese, the words mean "You are going to die."

At that moment, the world of mixed martial arts was split regarding Conor's chances of dethroning the only featherweight champion the UFC had ever known, but everyone agreed it would be his toughest test up to that point.

Conor didn't seem fazed.

He wasn't fazed two years earlier, either, when Jose's name was put to him in the lead-up to his UFC debut.

> *What, you think I'm afraid of him? Man, I would fight that guy in a heartbeat. I would fight any of them in a heartbeat. I will go forward, and I will go at them. There is no opponent. There's no Jose Aldo. Who the fuck is Jose Aldo? There's no no-one.* **You're against yourself.** *You know what*

———

I mean? You're against yourself. And I just feel like I'm able to beat myself. I can beat my mind. Do you know what I'm trying to say? I just believe in myself so much that nothing is going to stop me.

Conor McGregor, *The Rise of Conor McGregor*, MTV UK, March 7, 2013

SELF-MASTERY

You're against yourself. By embracing this idea, Conor is following the lead of some of the wisest men who have ever lived. Twenty-five hundred years ago, Plato wrote, "The first and best victory is to conquer the self." Five hundred years ago, Leonardo da Vinci wrote, "You will never have greater dominion than that over yourself. The height of a man's success is gauged by his self-mastery, the depth of his failure by his self-abandonment."

Conor's message is no different.

In anything the fight is won or lost in the mind. Your biggest opponent is yourself, and that is not just in combat sports, that is in anything.

Conor McGregor, Ireland AM on TV3, July 15, 2014

The true measure of any person's education is their self-mastery. Without this, all other education is good for next to nothing. Every individual must battle with and conquer themselves if they hope to attain their ideal. Even the most ambitious people

---

are often entangled by habits that cripple their efforts. They end up constantly struggling against themselves instead of working towards their goals.

Anyone who allows themselves to be controlled by their impulses and momentary desires will be limited in what they can achieve. Such people become so bound by their destructive behaviors that they hardly consider the possibility of freeing themselves. Gradually, they begin to accept the command of their lower self without opposition. They take for granted that they will always be at its mercy, that it is a necessary part of their existence. They go through life doing the small and trivial, when the grand and meaningful would be within their reach if they could liberate themselves.

It is only through deliberate efforts repeated day after day, week after week, month after month, that a person can work towards self-mastery. It is the greatest asset that can ever be acquired—the ability to fasten the mind securely to one's ambition, to the exclusion of everything else.

> *I don't have anything else going on. There's nothing else I do.* ***I don't do fuck-all else, other than this.*** *... And knowing that I have that kind of mentality—that's what gives me confidence.*
>
> Conor McGregor, *The Rise of Conor McGregor*, MTV UK, March 7, 2013

Conor hasn't always had the incredible work ethic to which he owes his success. It is precisely because self-mastery was so difficult for him that he identifies himself as his biggest opponent. There were many times early in Conor's career when he lost focus and came close to giving up on his dreams. There were many occasions when he struggled to, in his words, "stay on the straight and narrow."

Conor McGregor Shift Part 2, Bobby Razak, September 19, 2014

One of these times came shortly before he was signed by the UFC. Discouraged by a career-ending injury to one of his teammates, Conor stopped showing up at the gym and said to himself, "I don't think I wanna do this. Maybe this is not for me." A few weeks later, he was out with friends and got a series of calls from his coach, which he repeatedly ignored. When he finally gave in and answered, the first words he heard were, "How do you feel about making your UFC debut in nine weeks?"

Conor told this story on *The Fighter and The Kid* Podcast, March 27, 2015

No fight is more real than the one waged between an individual's higher and lower nature. There is a strong temptation at every stage of existence to sacrifice future goals for immediate pleasures. As Brian Tracy puts it in his book *No Excuses*, "Every day, and every minute of every day, there is a battle

---

---

going on inside of you between doing what is right, hard, and necessary or doing what is fun, easy, and of little or no value."

To move towards self-mastery, we must commit ourselves to winning more of these battles. We must exert whatever willpower is necessary to do the things we need to do whether we want to do them or not. However, self-mastery is ultimately about moving beyond the struggle—about learning how to enjoy the things that will unlock our highest ambitions.

Conor has shown exactly what this is like.

I enjoy work. I don't wanna be anywhere else.

Conor McGregor, UFC has Struck Gold, MMAFighting, May 29, 2015

The quality of mind necessary for a person to speak these words honestly is as rare as it is potent. Developing this mentality is only possible by setting out hearts firmly in the direction we mean to go— and then sacrificing every opposing desire. Such self-training, such self-conquest, gives a person great power.

I had a conversation with myself—"What are you here for? Why are you doing this? Are you gonna go all the way or are you gonna go half the way?"

Conor McGregor, UFC 194 LA Scrum, MMAFighting, September 2, 2015

HABITS

Given that self-mastery is about ending the struggle to do what we need to do, the best way to look towards achieving it is through the lens of our habits.

Habits are the actions we perform regularly with very little effort or conscious thought. The second part of that definition is what makes habits, both good and bad, so powerful. They are either our supreme strength or our most miserable weakness. We will become what we wish to become, do what we wish to do, only when our habits correspond with our goals. Carefully shaped, they allow us to perform automatically that which was so painful and difficult in our earlier efforts.

The video game *Call of Duty: Black Ops 2* came out on November 12, 2012. When Conor started playing the game, it became a habit that almost completely took over his life. Four years later, in an interview about his appearance as a character in one of the game's sequels, he described how addicted he had been to the game and the extent to which it had interfered with his training.

I was actually obsessed with this game. Call of Duty: Black Ops [2], *when that came out, I was in an apartment with my girlfriend, and I'd be*

---

literally up all night. She'd wake up at 6:30 a.m. to get ready to go to work, and I'd still be up playing the game, and when she'd wake up ... I'd go to sleep. ... And then off I'd go again—I'd go training for two hours and then I'd come back and I'd be playing the game all night until 6:30 a.m. That was a process I went through for a long while. I was actually hooked on the game.

Conor McGregor discusses Call of Duty, TheMacLife, November 4, 2016

This period in Conor's life came years after he went on record saying, "It's all or nothing in the game I'm in. If you're not training twice a day ... you're not gonna go anywhere." With this in mind, there can be no doubt that Conor was failing to live up to the standards he had set for himself.

Conor McGregor Before Fame, The Irish MMA Tapes, December 2008

Although we don't know when the exact moment was, Conor eventually left his video game addiction behind and rededicated himself to the study of mixed martial arts. The truth is that there is no single moment when everything comes together. Self-mastery is a process of constant rededication, one that often takes many years.

But if there is anything we should fight for, it is the ability to pursue our ideal, because in that is our greatest opportunity for self-expression. When starting on a journey so significant, we must first

---

---

remove every obstacle from our path. We must get absolute freedom from everything that chokes our ambitions and makes us satisfied with mediocrity. We must persistently, painfully, and with all the willpower we can summon, eliminate our bad habits and build new ones that will bring us to the future we desire.

> *There is no opponent. It's you versus you. ... Not even [just in] martial arts, [but in] life. It's always you versus you.*
>
> Conor McGregor, UFC on FUEL TV, Fighters Only, April 3, 2013

DESTROYING BAD HABITS

Every repetition of an act makes it more certain that it will be done again and again, quickly making the doer a slave. However, if we refuse to obey a certain habit, it will begin to expire. The longer we can go without giving in to the impulses to perform an action, the weaker those impulses will become.

The best assault on an unwanted habit is to abstain from it by whatever means necessary. Whenever possible, we should physically block our access to the activity. We should literally cut off our ability to engage in it until the power it has over us has weakened.

People often overestimate the capacity they have to

---

control their behavior through willpower alone. They do not understand that, despite their efforts, some old temptation could lure them in at an unguarded moment. Some old desire will flash across their mind, and they may find themselves submitting to the habits they thought had been conquered forever.

The only way for us to destroy a habit is to wrench ourselves away from it, to starve and neglect it, and to silence its voice immediately whenever it tries to call us back. Many people fail by allowing themselves to imagine returning to the behaviors they are trying so hard to erase. If we question our resolutions, temptation will grow and quickly take over our thoughts.

The consequences of indulging in our old habits are always worse than they seem. The most grievous damage is not merely the hours or days of wasted time, but the unraveling of our efforts to transform ourselves. Nothing but regret, disappointment, and disgust will follow.

The only person that can give you problems is the guy in the mirror.

Conor McGregor, The Time is Now Press Conference, November 17, 2014

If we are serious about reshaping our habits, we must set every possible condition that will reinforce our motive. We must make commitments that encourage new behaviors and cut off our access to those we are trying to discard. This will give our new beginning great momentum, and every day that we do not consider returning to our old habits increases the chances that we never will.

CREATING GOOD HABITS

To the same extent that the person plagued by bad habits is held back, the person with habits in alignment with their purpose is bound for success.

Forming the right habits is the best preparation for any achievement. If we are not prepared to capitalize on them, the opportunities that come our way will only make our failings all the more regrettable. Our preparation is more important than our opportunities. Our preparation *makes* our opportunities.

In the creation of a new habit, we must launch ourselves with as strong and decisive an initiative as possible. By forcing ourselves to repeat an action again and again, we can program into our minds a desire to carry out that action. As the habit grows stronger, the urge to perform it will come without thought.

Take exercising as an example. People who don't exercise often find it difficult to begin. But those who have formed the habit of exercising generally report that impulses to continue the routine come unconsciously. The habit can become so strong that people feel physically uncomfortable when they don't exercise. Conor has described many times that he now has to use his willpower *not* to train.

> *Whenever there's no media around, I find it hard to take a full day off. ... I say I'm gonna take a day off and then I take the day off and then it's midnight and I'm like, "Fuck it, I'm gonna go to the gym."*
>
> Conor McGregor, Hot 106.3 radio interview, November 20, 2014

The quality Conor indicates here—of being compulsively driven to do the kind of work that others cannot force themselves to do—is the result of using the mind's tendency towards repetition.

Whenever we're trying to develop a new habit, we should perform the desired action as often as possible—ideally every single day. We should not allow a single exception to occur until the behavior is deeply ingrained. However, this does not mean that each occasion must be long or intense. The formation of habit is much more about consistency than duration. In the early stages, we should focus less on the benefits of the action and more on the momentum created by performing it regularly.

There's nothing fancy about it. There's no secret to it.

You just show up every day, put the work in, and that's it. Reap the rewards.

Conor McGregor *Unfiltered*, Sports Illustrated, February 24, 2016

We must each create for ourselves the mentality that will lead us to success. Such a thing cannot be inherited. It cannot be purchased with money. It cannot be stumbled upon by chance. It is independent of birth, status, or wealth. It must be the outcome of our own decisions—the reward for determination and right action.

WILLPOWER

Willpower is what allows a person to force themselves to do something when they don't want to do it. It is one of the most important tools in the pursuit of self-mastery, but not in the way most people think.

Most people believe that maintaining changes in behavior requires the constant use of willpower. However, with the correct approach, willpower is necessary only in the beginning, as we destroy our bad habits and replace them with those that align with our goals. If we use our willpower wisely—*if we invest it* in reshaping our habits—we will reach a point at which we no longer have to rely on it to perform the desired actions.

Anyone who shifts into a new set of habits will

---

begin to take on the identities associated with those behaviors. As Tynan writes in *Superhuman by Habit*, "New habits are things that you do, but old habits are things that you are. There's a difference between waking up early and being an early riser, eating a healthy meal and being a healthy eater, getting some work done and being a productive person." The key difference is whether the action is forced through willpower or produced automatically through the power of habit.

We can make the will do our bidding and put it to any work we choose. The choices we make can mold us into cowards or heroes. They can lead us to laziness until every effort is disagreeable and success is impossible. Or they can hold us to our task until idleness and inaction are painful—until the qualities of success are built into our personality.

Lasting self-mastery can only be obtained gradually. How long the process takes depends on each person's individual mental constitution. But however long it takes, the acquisition of self-mastery is worth infinitely more than the effort it could ever cost.

YOU CAN HAVE ANYTHING YOU WANT,
IF YOU WANT IT BADLY ENOUGH.
YOU CAN BE ANYTHING YOU WANT TO BE,
DO ANYTHING YOU SET OUT TO ACCOMPLISH,
IF YOU HOLD TO THAT DESIRE
WITH SINGLENESS OF PURPOSE.

————

Conor's first step into martial arts was taken with purpose. He was ten years old, and his original purpose had nothing to do with passion, nothing to do with money, and nothing to do with world titles.

When I first got into combat sports, I didn't get in it to be a champion. ... I got in it because the kid across the street was gonna whoop my ass, so I wanted to prepare to whoop his ass if he came at me.

Conor McGregor with Jim Gray, SHOWTIME, August 24, 2017

The way a person responds to adversity—whether they cower and retreat or they set themselves to some productive action—instantly reveals the true nature of their character. Conor has said in interviews that when the need to defend himself first arose, he was "afraid of conflict." But by concentrating all his thoughts and actions on overcoming that fear, he started down a path that would lead him to self-discovery and stardom.

Fights would happen, but for me, it stuck in my head. Maybe if a fight happened another boy would have just left, and he would have

————

forgot completely about it, but for me I dwelled on it—"What way should I have moved there? He did this. Maybe if I had done that, it would have turned out better." … So it began to build in my mind that I wanted to become really good at this. I wanted to be able to defend myself in any situation, any movement, any scenario. So I went from gym to gym—kickboxing, boxing, grappling, wrestling—ultimately trying to learn different ways the body could move to attack and to defend.

Conor McGregor Exclusive, eir Sport, September 10, 2014

No matter what it is or how it's discovered, when a new and all-absorbing purpose like the one Conor describes first takes hold of a person, they instantly become something greater.

Everyone has more ability than they think they have, more than they will ever use under ordinary circumstances. There are many people who never discover what they are capable of until they feel cut off from outside resources, until it is clear that they must depend absolutely upon themselves. It is only when a strong enough motive presents itself—an emergency urgent enough, a responsibility heavy enough, an opportunity promising enough—that a person's hidden reserves are called out.

For Conor, this power was brought out by the need to defend himself from other kids in his neighborhood. His response not only allowed him to overcome the threat they represented, but also gave him an early understanding of what it means for a person to be fully committed to their goal.

Almost all of us have had these kinds of experiences in life—times when a crisis or deadline forced us to concentrate all our efforts on a single aim. Whatever the challenge, we found ourselves unusually driven and determined. Our minds became completely engaged in working towards the outcome we desired.

Such occasions offer a glimpse into a mindset that represents the pinnacle of human ability. Any time a crisis awakens in us that which we had not before utilized, it is an indication of our greater potential. If we could only make these productive times permanent, we would become more than we ever imagined.

The key to building this power into our lives is to create a sense of urgency that doesn't rely on external pressures. That is what Conor has done, and that is what he has in mind when he responds to questions about motivation by saying, "I am a self-motivated individual."

The Time is Now Press Conference, November 17, 2014

---

[25]

A decade after standing up for himself against the bullies on the block, Conor's purpose had evolved—from the externally motivated need to defend himself, to the internally motivated dream of becoming one of the greatest fighters of all time.

My dream is to be world lightweight champion in the UFC, have more money than I know what to do with, and have a great life for my kids and grandkids and everyone that's come up with me. **My dream is to be number one.**

Conor McGregor Before Fame, The Irish MMA Tapes, December 2008

Unless we are inspired by a resolute determination to make our lives count, we will never leave much of an impression on the world. Each of us ought to engage with that inner voice that urges us towards high achievement, even at the cost of our own comfort. It is only when we are driven by an ambition of our own choosing that we can have a true estimate of our ability.

The discovery of such a pursuit has the power to erase all discontent and drudgery from our lives. Once we truly dedicate ourselves to our vision, everything in our daily experience will be cast in a new light. The doubts, fears, and apathy that blighted our existence will all be dispelled by the positive energy of a new focus.

Conor's story is proof of this. His dedication to martial arts made his life better long before he achieved any fame or began earning enough money to support himself. The mere act of looking to the future with a stout determination had a great uplifting effect on him.

> **Martial arts gave me a purpose, gave me a dedication, gave me a drive that I wouldn't have had otherwise.** *What else am I gonna do? This is my life. This is the life I have chosen. I don't wanna be anywhere else but here. I'm a happy man right now. I'm living the dream.*
>
> Conor McGregor, Think Street Train Sport, FOX Sports, August 16, 2013

Conor's dream of becoming a UFC champion grew out of a passion for martial arts he'd been nurturing for years. Goals that can truly inspire us and help us evolve are usually derived from our passions. If we have nothing in our lives we are passionate about, our first purpose should be to find it.

> **Be passionate.**
>
> Conor McGregor, Twitter, February 12, 2014

PASSION

The most valuable thing that ever comes into any-one's life is that experience—that book, that person,

———————

that incident, that catastrophe, *that something—* which awakens in them a fascination that wasn't there before.

Many people make the mistake of thinking that having a passion like Conor's relies on an inborn quality. They believe that if they were meant to apply themselves to a particular craft, it would grab hold of their attention and force itself into their life.

Holding onto this belief will keep a person from ever fully expressing themselves. Passion is open and available to everyone. Once properly understood, it can be discovered and encouraged very easily.

> *There are avenues you can go where I come from. You can go one way and it's not a good way, or you can go another way and find a passion and focus on it.*

Conor McGregor, UFC 194 Lunch Scrum, MMAFighting, December 2, 2015

What is passion? For starters, it's one thing that helped Conor ascend to the top of the fight game. In the midst of Conor's rise, sports journalist Darren Frehill asked him, "What makes you such a good fighter?"

> *I'm just curious about it. I'm curious about it. I mean, it's in my head 24/7. I don't think about nothing else. And that's it. **I'm just curious—***

———————

---

curiously fascinated with it, and I can't stop thinking about it.

Conor McGregor, Darren Frehill, Jan 27, 2015

To be *curious* and *fascinated*—this is what it means to be passionate. Having a passion isn't just about being obsessed with something, it's about having an obsessive desire to learn and understand it.

Conor's emphasis on learning has been evident throughout his entire career. As he started head-lining his first events, earning his first six-figure paychecks, and taking strides towards winning his first UFC championship, Conor made it clear that his attention remained entirely focused on mastering his craft.

Through all the other shit, it's about getting better. Nothing else matters except me showing up at the gym every single day and putting in the work to get better—to get a better understanding of movement, to get a better understanding of this game. Everything else means nothing.

Conor McGregor Exclusive, eir Sport, September 10, 2014

This is what true passion sounds like. At the root of all passion is the desire to learn. Anyone who is interested in understanding how things work can discover new passions very easily. It is only those afflicted with an attitude of indifference who are

---

condemned to find the world dull and uninspiring.

When Conor tells people to "be passionate," he is telling them to be curious and fully engaged with life. No other advantage can replace these qualities. A person may lack many important things and yet still achieve a great deal if they have mental intensity—the ability to focus all their energy on one thing.

You gotta be serious. You gotta be switched-on. So I'm switched-on one hundred percent, 24/7, all day, everyday. I'm switched. My mind is on this.

Conor McGregor, UFC 194 Lunch Scrum, MMAFighting, December 2, 2015

Anyone who wishes to develop a passion must begin by choosing to be interested in the world. Few people realize the extent to which this lies within their control. Whether something is trivial or meaningful depends largely on the spirit with which we take hold of it. It is possible to elevate even the most ordinary task by approaching it with the curiosity and fascination of a master.

Although Conor's passion for unarmed combat became a career for him, we don't have to begin each endeavor believing it will be what we do for the rest of our lives. It is very rare for a person to do the same thing in the same way for their entire life. Most people who succeed combine different strengths gathered from different pursuits to create something unique and of their own.

Conor often speaks about the benefits that training martial arts can offer to those who use it to improve themselves.

> *The martial arts life will give you a discipline, will give you a dedication, will give you a drive that you won't get nowhere else. So whatever these kids that come in [from a young age] decide to do—whether they decide to conquer the martial arts world, the fighting game, or whether they wanna go and conquer the business world. Whatever they decide to do, training for combat sports, training in martial arts, will give them that confidence to go and excel in anything.*

Conor McGregor Exclusive, eir Sport, September 10, 2014

Every pursuit offers its own benefits, and any passion can be used as a vehicle for growth. The important thing is to throw ourselves into *something*, to fling our whole lives into it.

Once a person has discovered an interest, they should do everything they can to give energy to it, to explore it as deeply as possible and see how far they can take it. Interests do not develop into passions on their own. They must be cultivated through conscious decision-making and deliberate effort.

Passion often calls for attention very early in a person's life. But if they do not heed its voice, if it gets no encouragement after appealing to them for years, it gradually ceases to call. Like any other quality, it will deteriorate and disappear if unused. There is always hope for a person as long as their passion is alive, but when that has left them, their greatest impelling motive is lost.

Regardless of how ambitious we plan to be with our passion, it is imperative that we find in it some overriding goal. The thing that makes a person's life distinctive is the one supreme thing they are trying to accomplish. It is only when the mind is stretched towards a specific objective that it begins to uncover its true potential.

I feel what your passion can do—your passion opens up avenues that you can take. And it's important to go down that avenue at a hundred miles an hour, take full advantage of every avenue that opens.

Conor McGregor, UFC 189 World Tour Dublin, SevereMMA, March 31, 2015

PURPOSE
The person who succeeds has a purpose. They set their course and adhere to it. They lay their plans and execute them. They are not pushed around

whenever an obstacle is thrown in their path or a temptation seeks to rob them of their time.

What leads to achievement is not so much brilliancy of intellect and vastness of resources, but persistency of effort and constancy of purpose. A person may be poor and have nobody to push them or encourage them, but if they have a strong enough will they can defy the world.

> *To reach the high pinnacle of your game, of your love, of your passion, **everything else must not exist**. And that is the way it is for me.*
>
> Conor McGregor, Welcome to my Office, MMAWeekly, September 24, 2014

Once we have chosen a worthy goal, it becomes the engine that makes all the hard work and sacrifice possible. It becomes the reason for summoning all our powers of focus and initiative, for conquering everything holding us back.

Without a clear ambition in mind, we are not severe enough with ourselves, not demanding enough. There must be some greater meaning behind our efforts, some master aim to strive towards. What we do begrudgingly without a purpose, with a purpose becomes our highest pleasure. It is just that added element that makes our work feel immortal.

After Conor won his first UFC fight, when his

years of training were just beginning to pay off, he was asked about the "tough times" he had on his journey to turn his passion into a career.

> *There's tough times either way. There's tough times for everyone. There's tough times when you're doing your stupid little job that you hate every minute of, and there's tough times when you're broke while you're chasing your dream. Don't dwell on that.* **Just pursue what you love. Do what you love.**

Conor McGregor, Balls on the Ground, Balls.ie, July 30, 2013

The world always makes way for those who know their ideal and stick to it with a strength of purpose from which nothing can move them. When a person's ambition is so ingrained into their character that you can't get them away from it without killing them—without taking their life along with their purpose—their success is inevitable.

After Conor described the intensity of his curiosity and fascination, he was asked if he thought it was unhealthy to be so focused on one thing.

> *Do I look unhealthy? Take a look at this physique. I'm in phenomenal shape—in body and mind. To me what's unhealthy is living an unhealthy life. To me what's unhealthy is getting up and going through the same day every day of your life, nine*

———

to five in an office. ... That's unhealthy. That beats your mind. I don't work. I love what I do, and that's why I'm doing what I love. That's why it's become a career for me—because I love it. I love what I do. So, I don't think it's unhealthy. I feel good in my mind. It's my life.

Conor McGregor, Darren Frehill, Jan 27, 2015

———

I BELIEVED IT WAS GOING TO HAPPEN,
I PUT THE WORK IN FOR IT TO HAPPEN,
AND IT HAPPENED.

Kneeling on the canvas and clutching a balled-up, blood-stained Irish flag after winning his first UFC championship fight, Conor McGregor showed on his face what it meant to him to achieve the goal he'd been working towards for over a decade.

In an interview during the buildup to the event, Conor was asked what it is that makes him better than other fighters. His answer was simple and to the point.

> *My belief. I have a belief in myself that nobody can stop me.*
>
> Conor McGregor, If the Division Begs, MMAJunkie, March 23, 2015

People are always asking Conor about his self-belief. He earned the nickname 'Mystic Mac' while gutting the featherweight division with a string of knockouts he'd predicted beforehand. He's one of the only fighters who even attempts to call his shots, and he's by far the most accurate.

But Conor's confidence runs deeper than the habit he has of looking opponents dead in the eye and telling them what he will do to them. The most compelling examples of his self-belief come from

---

much earlier in his career. They are the beliefs he held from the very beginning—long before he had made believers of many others.

By the end of 2008, Conor had earned himself a professional record of 3-1. At twenty years old, he was just completing his first year of full-time training, but was already prophesying his future UFC success with the same conviction he has today.

> I will—*I will*—be where I wanna be. I'm one hundred percent confident of that—that I will make it to the top. I have the skills, I have the dedication, and it's something I really, really want. Words can't even describe, but it will happen, and I'll let you know when it happens.

Conor McGregor Before Fame, The Irish MMA Tapes, December 2008

Over the next four years, Conor would decide that making it to the top wasn't ambitious enough. Days before his UFC debut, Conor recorded a new prediction of what he would accomplish. He was not merely going to become a UFC champion, he was going to transform the world of combat sports.

> I believe I can be a national hero and change the way people from Ireland and people all over the world look at combat ... change the definition of what a fighter is, of what a combat sports star is.

Conor McGregor, UFC Stockholm, Tiam Kakavand, April 4, 2013

Conor has proven time after time his ability to forecast the future. He has not only ascended to the top of the fight game, but has redefined what it means to be at the top. To fully understand how dauntless this second prediction was when he made it, consider this: Just a few days before recording those words, Conor picked up a welfare check on his way to the airport.

Two years later, weeks after Conor won his first UFC belt, sports journalist Gareth Davies reminded him of the financial hardship he went through, of the years he spent training and fighting before it began to pay off. Gareth then asked him if he had faith back then that his time would come.

Conor leaned forward and smiled as if he were divulging a little-known secret.

> *If I didn't, it wouldn't have happened. I had to believe in it, I had to feel it, I had to have faith in it—for it to happen. So, you're damn right I did.*

Conor McGregor, UFC 194 Interview, BT Sport, November 10, 2015

What Conor's getting across is that self-belief isn't just something that's nice to have. It's not an accessory. It is the foundation of all achievement—the forerunner that goes ahead and clears the way for all the other faculties of the mind.

It is tempting to believe that Conor's confidence

is just a part of his personality, but he and his coach have put deliberate effort into creating an atmosphere of absolute belief in the inevitability of their success. They figured out very early on that what an individual is capable of depends largely on what they think of themselves and their possibilities.

> *[John] builds my confidence up and makes me feel like I'm better than I am without me actually knowing that he's trying to do that. Not too forward, but building up my confidence on a subliminal level. That's what a good coach can do.*
>
> Conor McGregor, The Dugout, Three Ireland, June 11, 2013

A fight is one of the most challenging trials a person can experience. To be exhausted and caught in a vulnerable, painful position is to have every reason to give up hope and find a way out. Fighters must train themselves never to lose confidence in their ability to overcome the challenges presented to them by their opponents.

But here's the thing: The impulses to quit that fighters face over the fifteen or twenty-five minutes of an MMA bout are also confronted in the weeks, months, and years spent working towards *any* goal. The constant discouragements we encounter in life bring great temptations to lower our standards and abandon our dreams. When we face such trials, we will be armed only with the belief and determination we have developed beforehand.

The answer's not out there, my friend. The answer's in here, in your heart, in your belief.

Conor McGregor, UFC 178 Media Day, MMAWeekly, September 26, 2014

Most people are weaker in confidence than in any other aspect. They limit themselves with their thoughts. They neutralize a large part of their efforts because their attitude does not support their endeavor. Any glimmer of ambition they have is overshadowed by a self-doubt that urges them towards mediocrity.

Success is impossible for anyone who allows fear to hold them back, who hesitates, who is never sure of themselves, who feels they must seek out the opinions of others as to what they can achieve. Fear is one of the greatest enemies of a person's advancement. It suggests caution at the moment everything depends on boldness.

If you limit your choices only to what seems possible or reasonable, you disconnect yourself from what you truly want, and all that is left is a compromise.

Conor McGregor quoting Robert Fritz, *Notorious*, RTÉ, March 13, 2014

People of courage and action can take wrong

steps and make mistakes—sometimes serious ones. But in a lifetime they accomplish far more than the timid, negative individual who has not enough belief in themselves to trust in their potential. It is almost always the person with absolute faith in their ability that prevails. Their confidence, their conviction, their positive expectation are all powerful factors in the securing of their ambition.

THOUGHT AND SPEECH

After a year of build up and anticipation, Conor's fight against Jose Aldo took place on December 12, 2015. With the second punch he threw, Conor landed a left-hand counter that rendered Aldo completely unconscious. The bout lasted just 13 seconds—the shortest championship fight in UFC history.

Two days before Conor became the undisputed featherweight champion, he went on record with his forecast of how the fight would go. At the UFC 194 post-fight press conference, MMA analyst Robin Black read Conor's prediction back to him:

Word-for-word, you said: *I felt when we stared down, I felt his right hand was twitching, which was a subtle tell for me. He is ready to unload that right hand, and I feel that could be a downfall*

---

for him. If he lets that right hand go, I will not be there. I simply enter the way I enter, and that is enough. They either overextend or they shrink away, but either way, it is not good for them. I will create traps and dead space inside that octagon, and I will walk him into that dead space. But all of a sudden he will be in danger.

Black then asked his question: "How do you do that? How do you predict these things?"

A big grin had spread across Conor's face. He pointed to his temple.

If you can see it here, and you have the courage enough to speak it, it will happen. I see these shots. I see these sequences. And I don't shy away from them. A lot of times people believe in certain things, but they keep to themselves. They don't put it out there. If you truly believe in it, if you become vocal with it, you are creating that law of attraction, and it will become reality.

Conor McGregor, UFC 194 Post-Fight Press Conference, December 12, 2015

Every thought that runs through a person's mind has the power to contribute to or detract from shaping the reality they desire. Whatever we think about ourselves, whatever we choose to believe about our possibilities, is constantly reinforcing an atmosphere of either success or failure.

The distance between doubt and belief, between hesitancy and decision, between 'I'll try' and 'I will' is equal to the distance between weakness and power, between mediocrity and excellence, between commonness and superiority.

Conor takes the power of self-belief to its absolute limits. He admits that at times he has even convinced himself of things that did not match reality.

> *[If] you tell yourself, "OK, I'm Number Two," well then you're Number Two.* **I tell myself I'm Number One.** *I was telling myself that when I was probably Number Ninety-Two. ... Now I am Number One. I just keep that belief. ... It's all in the head, it really is.*
>
> Conor McGregor, Norik Koczarian, September 30, 2013

No conduct can get a person to their goal while their mind is working against them. Negativity kills determination, destroys ambition, ruins hopes and plans. It makes us traitors to the things we long to do.

Whenever a person's confidence is weak, their will becomes weak. No matter what our goals, we must do everything we can to remain positive in our mentality. We must strangle all ideas of doubt and see every obstacle we encounter as part of a story that will end in our success.

There is nothing arrogant about carrying the self-perception that maximizes our chance of victory. There is nothing rude in the assertion that we will succeed where others have failed. Whatever the mind is filled with, it attracts. If it is filled with the dread of failure, it invites defeat. But if it is filled with optimism, with the sincere expectation of good things, it will make those things more likely.

> *I am cocky in prediction, I am confident in preparation, but I am always humble—in victory or defeat.*

Conor McGregor, UFC 178 Post-Fight Press Conference, September 27, 2014

The person with absolute faith in their abilities is almost always the one most likely to triumph. They deal in affirmations. They throw themselves with conviction into their quest, never harboring any doubt that they can do what they undertake. And the result is often what they have trained themselves to expect—they succeed in what they attempt.

> *Through years in the gym—through wins, through losses, through life—I just realized that if you say it to yourself, and you look yourself in the eye ... and truly believe that not a man alive can beat you, then that is the way it is.*

Conor McGregor, UFC 183 Q&A, January 30, 2014

VISUALIZATION

Visualization is one of the most well-researched techniques in the psychology of success. Any time a person visualizes the future as they would like it to be, they strengthen their ability to bring that vision into reality.

Conor has been using the tool of visualization for his entire career. Days before Conor's first UFC main event in Dublin, MMA journalist Ariel Helwani asked him if he visualized himself as a star back when he was broke and struggling to work towards his dream.

> *Of course, because you have to do that. You have to battle with this. This is the law of attraction. When things are going good and you visualize more good things happening, that's easy. What's not easy is to do it when things are going bad ... and that was what I was able to do. Even though [my situation wasn't good], I still was able to feel like it was. Just like a kid would use his imagination. I was basically just using my imagination.*

Conor McGregor, A Day in Dublin, MMAFighting, July 17, 2014

Every achievement has its origin in the mind. The accomplishments of all successful people are always the realized visions of their past selves— their dreams of bettering themselves and their

---

circumstances. The vivid and confident mental planning of one's goal sets all of the subconscious processes of the mind into action.

> *I see myself as the champ already. I saw myself as the champ from day one. ... That's how I see myself. I visualize myself already there. I visualize everything. I visualize this conversation. I visualize the walkout. ... I've seen everything in my head, and now it's going to happen. **You see it in your head, you're gonna see it before your eyes.***
>
> Conor McGregor, *The MMA Hour 170*, February 26, 2013

Visualizing is simply a matter of thinking about an event using senses rather than words. It is one of the best ways to prepare the mind for future goals and challenges. We should always do the four following things when visualizing:

1. See the vision through our own eyes, from our own perspective, not looking at ourselves from the outside.
2. Engage as many senses as possible.
3. Be precise. Who's there? What's happening? How does it feel? What unexpected things could happen? How will we overcome those things?
4. See the vision through to the end with the outcome we're working towards.

Conor has also spoken about using the past as a template for visualizing the future.

A couple weeks after the fight, I watch the whole thing, and I go back there. ... I like to do that a lot. It's like mental preparation. Even if I'm not there, I go to that place where I was feeling those feelings. I live there. So when [I'm actually there], it's just another day. I'm so comfortable with it. I'm so used to it.

Conor McGregor, *Notorious*, Universal Studios, November 1, 2017

We must believe that our heart's longings are something more than imagination and idle dreams. We must see them as forerunners of what is in our reach, as prophecies of what is in store for us.

An individual can have no greater self-protection from all that is low and ordinary than carrying a grand estimate of themselves and their possibilities. All people who achieve great things are dreamers. What they accomplish is in proportion to the clarity with which they see their vision, and the persistency with which they struggle to make it come true.

I always visualized good things. I always visualized victory, success, abundance. I visualized it all and it's all happening.

Conor McGregor, UFC 194 LA Scrum, MMAFighting, September 2, 2015

ACTION

Purposeful action and self-belief feed off each other. Neither can survive without the other. Whenever we make progress towards our goal, we instantly reinforce the belief that we will succeed. And if we are convinced that the reality we are striving for is possible, we will be more willing to put in the work necessary to attain it.

Hardly an interview goes by without Conor emphasizing the importance of hard work, often citing it as the primary source of his confidence. Less than a week before Conor won his second UFC belt at Madison Square Gardens, ESPN's Zubin Mehenti asked him about his unique mindset: "Conor, we've covered so many athletes over the years at ESPN. I can't remember an athlete that has the level of confidence you do. Where does that come from?"

> *[My confidence] comes from my work ethic. I work extremely hard in this business. I have dedicated my entire life to this craft. ... And that's it. **I gain confidence through my work.***

> Conor McGregor, ESPN SportsCenter, November 10, 2016

Without doing what is necessary to succeed, true self-belief is impossible. It is only when belief crystallizes into the resolve to do what is required that it has any weight. Dreaming when we have the determination to match those dreams with action is a grand thing. But dreaming without effort, wishing without the willingness to do everything in our power to realize the wish, is merely fantasizing.

I'm a dreamer.

Conor McGregor, UFC 189 Press Conference, July 9, 2015

When Conor re-injured his knee in the lead-up to UFC 189, he faced something that would have made nearly every other fighter on the roster pull out of the contest. But his ability to overcome that challenge (and the challenge of a new opponent, as Jose Aldo pulled out of their fight with a bruised rib) fueled his self-belief even more.

*My confidence is going [through the roof] because I faced adversity. The true greats can conquer adversity, and that's what I said to myself every day in that camp: "**The true greats come through adversity. They cut through adversity like a chainsaw through butter.**" That's what I kept saying to myself every day, and I came through it. And now my confidence is through the roof.*

Conor McGregor, UFC 194 LA Scrum, MMAFighting, September 2, 2015

Most people fail because there is no energy in their purpose, no strength in their resolutions. They peter out after a few setbacks, not realizing

———

that success in anything is the result of tremendous resolve, vigorous self-belief, and work, work, work. Half-hearted efforts and weak resolutions have never yet accomplished anything great and never will.

There are times when we cannot see the way ahead, when we seem to be completely enveloped in the fogs of fear and doubt. But we can always do the thing that will keep us moving forward—continue to work towards our goal whether it is in sight or not. This is the only chance we have of overcoming our difficulties.

You just have to outwork that fear, outwork that doubt.

Conor McGregor, A Day in Dublin, MMAFighting, July 17, 2014

———

NEVER FEAR DEFEAT.
DEFEAT IS THE SECRET INGREDIENT TO SUCCESS.

*Y*ou don't lose. You win, or you learn.

Conor McGregor, Off the Ball, March 27, 2014

Inside the walls of Straight Blast Gym Dublin, the phrase "win or learn" represents an attitude so essential to the success of Conor McGregor and his team that head coach John Kavanagh wrote a book with those three words as the title—*Win or Learn: MMA, Conor McGregor, and Me.*

In a conversation at the book launch, John explained what the phrase means to him and how it affects the way he coaches his fighters and those who train with him.

> *My philosophy in life is win or learn. I've tried to create a gym environment where people are not afraid to fail ... because they understand that loss is an absolutely necessary step on the way to becoming successful.*

John Kavanagh, *Win or Learn* Book Launch, MMAConnectTV, June 28, 2016

Conor's embracing of his coach's philosophy has helped get him through the darkest times of his career. After capturing the 145-pound world title, Conor was scheduled for a 155-pound contest against then-champion Rafael Dos Anjos. A win against Dos Anjos would have secured Conor's long-time goal of being the first person ever to hold two UFC belts in two weight divisions simultaneously.

Conor didn't get that opportunity. Less than two weeks before the event, Dos Anjos suffered a broken foot and was forced to pull out of the contest. After the withdrawal, Conor switched from one unprecedented challenge to another, accepting late-replacement Nate Diaz for a fight at 170 pounds, 25 pounds up from where Conor was champion.

Having entered the contest as a 4:1 favorite, and having dominated the first round, Conor's second-round loss by rear naked choke was both unexpected and devastating. At the post-fight press conference, Conor described himself as "heartbroken," but the attitude instilled in him by his coach elevated his mindset and allowed him to deal with the loss productively.

*I will never shy away from a challenge. I will never shy away from defeat. ... **We can either run from adversity, or we can face our adversity head-on and conquer it**, and that's what I plan to do. ... I'll face it. ... I'll learn from it.*

Conor McGregor, UFC 196 Post-Fight Press Conference, March 5, 2016

The way Conor carried himself on the night of the

loss brought him an immense amount of respect from the world of mixed martial arts. As media and fans reacted to the fight, it became clear that his composure in the face of defeat had earned him more esteem than another win likely would have. As eight-time MMA journalist of the year Ariel Helwani put it, "I was almost more impressed with him in defeat than I ever was in victory. He walked out, held his head very high, made no excuses, spoke very honestly about his performance and the situation, and I think he gained a lot more fans in doing so."

The world cannot help but admire an individual who grows hungrier as they grapple with adversity— who springs forth from every setback eager to show their courage and resilience. There is something in the determination of one who never gives up that instantly earns our respect. There is something grand and inspiring about a person who fails after giving their utmost and then enters the contest a second time, undaunted and with redoubled energy.

Few things seem impossible for the person who never weakens under trials or defeats, who pushes forward when everyone else has surrendered, who gets up with greater resolve each time they are knocked down. Anyone who can smile confidently when everything has just gone against them shows that they have the makings of greatness, for no ordinary person can do this.

Days after Conor swore he would face his adversity, a rematch with Nate Diaz was already in the works. And although both his coach and UFC president Dana White tried to get him to do the second fight at 155 pounds, Conor demanded that it be at the same weight as their first fight. In the lead-up to the rematch, Conor was asked why he was so adamant about having it at 170 pounds, even though both fighters came from lighter divisions.

> *I couldn't make it at any other weight except the weight that I was defeated at. It would have raised questions. I feel it would have defeated the purpose of what this is about. ... I just wanted to keep it as is—have my training camp and preparation for that frame, for that larger man. I wanted no changes.*
>
> Conor McGregor, UFC 202 Media Day, August 12, 2016

Conor's resolve would pay off at UFC 202, where he avenged his loss in a bloody, back-and-forth, five-round decision. From the first questions he was asked following the defeat at UFC 196, Conor maintained that he had "absolutely no regrets" about accepting the short-notice fight and that he "enjoyed the fact that [Nate] could take [his punches] and keep coming." When Conor had exacted his revenge and spoke about the two fights afterwards, he continued to express gratitude for the way everything had played out.

> *I'm happy [the fight with Rafael Dos Anjos didn't happen] because [the loss] allowed me to grow as a fighter. I took on a challenge that excited me. That second Diaz fight excited me. I came alive for it. I put in everything for it. And I grew as a man and as a fighter.*
>
> Conor McGregor, Mystic Mac Predicts, UFC, November 9, 2016

Just days after speaking those words, Conor would capture the lightweight title from Eddie Alvarez, making history as the first person to ever hold two UFC belts at the same time.

> *You brush it off and you come back.* ***Defeat is the secret ingredient to success.***
>
> Conor McGregor, mixedmartialarts.com, October 16, 2014

It is what a person does after suffering a loss, rather than before, that is their true measure. The most marked characteristic of those who leave the greatest impression on the world is loyalty to their ambition. Countless individuals have broken through the doors of success simply by pushing ahead where others have turned back.

CONOR MCGREGOR

———

The person who conquers is the one that keeps working steadily towards their goal, not bothering to check if their goal is always in sight. Anyone who is so devoted to their aim that they never consider quitting will be immune to many of the things that hold back those with a half-committed purpose.

One person merely 'desires' to do this or that, or 'wishes' they could, or 'would be glad' if they could. Another knows perfectly well that, if they live long enough, they will do the thing they set their heart on. They will not be discouraged. They will lose no time in putting forth all their energy to make it real.

Too many people, when they're trying to do something, maybe start a new business or whatever, and on the first pitfall, they say, "I guess I'm not good enough—it's not for me." ... Some people take a loss and it really knocks them out, and they're done. [Others] take a loss and turn it around and sit back after it and think about it and say, "What did I do wrong? What could I do better? Who should I be listening to? Where can I learn? How can I move on?" And it's those people who go on to become successful.

John Kavanagh, *Win or Learn* Book Launch, MMAConnectTV, June 28, 2016

Although Conor's defeat at UFC 196 took place

———

on one of the biggest stages possible, a person's resilience doesn't only reveal itself in those kinds of high-stakes situations. It applies to every aspect of our lives, determining how we respond to the most trivial inconveniences and the biggest, most challenging opportunities. It affects how we think, speak, and act, as well as how others think, speak, and act towards us.

Some see failure as revealing to the world they aren't good enough; others see failure as an opportunity to learn and improve. Some feel threatened by those who are better than them; others feel inspired. Some recoil from challenges and run from adversity; others run *towards* adversity because they know it is the only way to bring out the best things in themselves.

The loss against Nate Diaz that broke Conor's fifteen-fight winning streak was his first in the UFC, but it was not the first time he had to overcome a setback after being signed to the organization. On August 17, 2013, during a dominant win over future champion Max Holloway, Conor suffered a torn ligament in his knee that would sideline him for eleven months.

In his book *Win or Learn*, John recalls what he said to Conor to help him mentally prepare to

---

overcome the injury:

Conor, champions conquer all adversity. That's what separates them from the challengers. There's been adversity in the past, there's adversity right now, and there'll be even more adversity in the future. But you've overcome it before and you're going to overcome it again. Why? Because you're on the road to becoming a UFC champion and this is just a minor obstacle along the way. This time next year we're going to be laughing about all of this.

John Kavanagh, *Win or Learn*, June 30, 2016

Conor took the encouragement to heart. With John's guidance, he would make a competition out of his comeback, vowing to return from the injury faster than anyone had before. When asked about the injury on episode 200 of *The MMA Hour*, Conor stated that, "This is just a new phase in my story ... another chapter that I will overcome."

The ability to right one's mind in the face of despair is a quality of all those who have achieved greatness. We must know ourselves and allow nothing—no combination of adversity or misfortune to bar our way. We must commit ourselves to what we're after with such determination that no force in the world can pull us away from it.

———

Most people are unable to see the things they begin through to the end. They can make a sudden dash and continue as long as everything goes smoothly, but they are easily disheartened. Discouragement wilts them. Misfortune robs them of their courage. It is the person who resolves to succeed and then who at every new challenge begins resolutely again that ends up victorious.

After the fight that followed Conor's knee injury and lengthy recovery—a first-round TKO victory in his hometown—he discussed the triumph of overcoming the injury:

> *I always had the belief that I was gonna return, and not only return, return better than anybody has ever returned before. Many people have torn their ACL and returned to combat, but not many people have returned better than they left, and I returned better than I left. ... If anything they come back the same, if not a little bit worse. I came back throwing shots that I've never thrown before. **It was all a blessing in disguise.***

Conor McGregor Exclusive, eir Sport, September 10, 2014

A blessing in disguise. Conor is only able to use these words to describe such a significant injury because of the decisions he made afterwards. It is not some mysterious outside force that transforms a

———

---

catastrophe into a blessing, but a person's reaction. Whenever we can use something we regret as a catalyst for something constructive, we have conquered that regret. Taking productive action can turn almost all forms of loss, failure, and disappointment into something positive.

It is useless to oppose anyone who uses their setbacks as stepping stones. Such a person cannot be talked down. Defeat cannot dishearten them. Misfortune cannot deter them. Hardship cannot turn them a hair's breadth from their course. No matter what opposition or discouragement they encounter, they keep their eye on their purpose and push on.

I feel strong. I feel strong in my mind. I always do. **I don't let defeat faze me.** *Like I said before, the true champions can come back. The true champions rise again, and I am a true champion.*

Conor McGregor, UFC 202 Media Day, MMAFighting, August 13, 2016

SINGLENESS OF PURPOSE

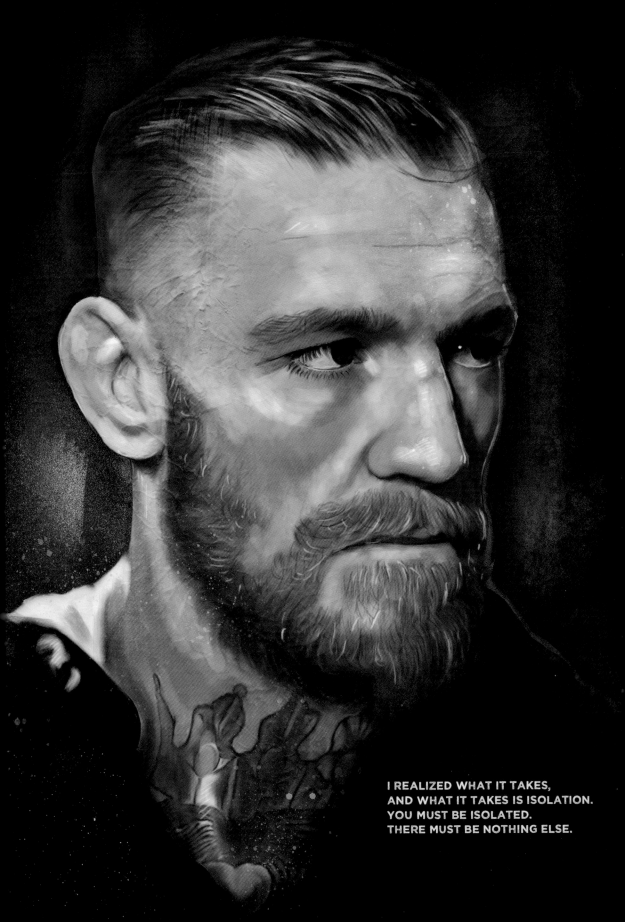

I REALIZED WHAT IT TAKES,
AND WHAT IT TAKES IS ISOLATION.
YOU MUST BE ISOLATED.
THERE MUST BE NOTHING ELSE.

One of the best things to happen to Conor, one of the most critical detours his journey took, was something he resisted as it occurred. After living in Crumlin, Dublin for the first sixteen years of his life, Conor's family uprooted and moved to Lucan, another Dublin suburb fifteen kilometers west from the neighborhood he grew up in. Opposed to the change at the time, Conor later realized how crucial it was for him to get away from the people holding him back.

> *When I moved from Crumlin to Lucan when I was [sixteen], **that was a life-saver for me**, because I moved away from everything. While everyone else was getting caught up in stuff, I got away. ... I was literally sitting in a room on my own. But I was with myself and my thoughts a lot at that time ... just going to the gym in Rathcoole and then home to Lucan. I had nothing else to do, so it helped me.*
>
> Conor McGregor Exclusive, eir Sport, September 10, 2014

For Conor to describe leaving his friends and everything he was familiar with as a "life-saver" speaks to how pivotal the move was for him. And

---

while it's impossible to know what would have become of him without the fresh start and the time it gave him to focus on his passion, it seems fair to say he wouldn't be where he is today.

But for every person like Conor who escapes the negative influences dragging them down, there are many others who never do. There are many who repeat the same destructive patterns for decades, while all their passions and ambitions starve to death. What these people need more than anything else is to break free from these patterns, to erase from their life everything that lowers their standards and distracts them from their goals.

> *I feel to be at the pinnacle of any game ... you've got to be a little bit gone to it—you're not all there. You've gotta be almost insane to your craft. Not a lot of people can understand that. That's why I don't know about nothing else. I do not pay attention to nothing else. There were games of football on yesterday, there was rugby, there was this, there was that. And normal society is like, "Let's talk about this. Let's engage in this," and I just can't do it.*

Conor McGregor, UFC 194 Interview, BT Sport, November 10, 2015

There is great power in a resolution without reservations—a strong, persistent purpose that

---

[66]

_____

clears all obstacles from its path no matter how long it may take, no matter what the sacrifice or cost. It takes a stout ambition and a firm resolve to free oneself from all of life's trivialities—to become almost entirely ignorant of everything but the requirements of one's goal.

> *With all due respect, I fucking hate everything else. I just don't have time for it.*
>
> Conor McGregor, *Notorious* TV series, RTÉ, January 26, 2015

Most people are too easy on themselves, too timid, too willing to drift with the tide of their impulses. Moving forward in life is a process of choosing between the worthless and the worthwhile. Anyone who hopes to succeed where others have failed must begin with the ability to say 'No' where others have said 'Yes.'

Growing up in Ireland, Conor played soccer and even had dreams of competing professionally before the need to defend himself led him to combat sports. In a 2014 interview, he was asked if he was still a fan of soccer.

> *Funnily enough, not anymore. But I don't know what I was a fan of, because you just grow up into these things. It's kind of forced on you, like the way American football is forced on [Americans], and baseball, and all these other crap sports—__they are__*

_____

---

forced on you. ... As I grew up, I realized "This football is a bit shit. I'd rather be able to whoop somebody's ass." ... In Ireland and the UK football is huge. You jump into a taxi, and they'll be like, "Did you see the game?"—[I say] "No, I didn't see the game. I don't watch the game."

Conor McGregor, Welcome to my Office, MMAWeekly, September 24, 2014

The process Conor describes here—of detaching himself from the things culture forced on him and told him were important—was absolutely critical to his success.

One of the main reasons so many fail is that they do not go all-in. They are not willing to forgo their little pleasures, to give up their trivial diversions for the sake of a larger future. They are not willing to spend their free time on self-improvement, on educating and fitting themselves masterfully for their purpose.

I don't think about nothing else except this. I can't even sit through a movie without drifting off ten minutes in and I'm in half-guard-top, trying to pass half-guard and secure a more dominant position. And next thing you know, the film is half over and I haven't a clue what's going on. So, I'm just in my little bubble right now to obtain gold.

Conor McGregor, UFC Dublin Press Conference, KammakazeTV, July 16, 2014

Life's prospects are far greater for anyone with the courage to burn all bridges back to their old habits and negative influences. The trouble with so many of us is that we form our plans with meekness instead of determination—without the willingness to make sacrifices and master temptations. We may say we desire success, but we do not take the time to create the life conditions of the successful. Anyone who hopes to reach their ideal must let the single purpose they have chosen for themselves stand like iron bars against everything else.

> *I can't function around normal society or talk about normal things because I'm just off somewhere else.* **I'm just deep in my craft, and there's no going back.** *And I'm happy with that. I chose to do that.*
>
> Conor McGregor, UFC 196 Open Workout Scrum, MMAFighting, March 2, 2016

Everywhere we see people doing small, trivial things when they have within them great possibilities. Either they do not take their lives seriously, or there is just enough doubt and uncertainty regarding their success to take the edge off their efforts. And it is this difference—between going half-way and throwing all of themselves into their endeavor—that makes the difference between mediocrity and grand achievement.

———

Conor's move at sixteen wasn't the only occasion he benefited from being removed from what was familiar to him. After tearing a ligament in his knee during his second UFC fight, Conor spent months in Los Angeles doing rehab. He would recognize this as another instance in which he was helped by being cut off from temptation.

I can be a product of my environment. If I'm with the wrong crowd, I just become—whatever. That's why I like to be isolated. That's why this has helped me—coming out [to LA] and being locked in an apartment on my own. Building back up my leg—going from rehab to home, to rehab to home. Because there were no outsiders. ... There was nothing else going on in my life. ... **To get to the pinnacle, it needs to be like that. It needs to be no outsiders. You need to have your team and your focus and that's it.**

Conor McGregor *Shift* Part 2, Bobby Razak, September 19, 2014

Both apathy and ambition are contagious. No matter how strong our will, we will always take hold of the spirit that dominates in our surroundings. It will make all the difference if we are with people who encourage and inspire us, rather than with those who throw temptations in our path and distract us from our purpose.

———

People are either doing one of two things—they're adding to, or they're subtracting from. ... Over the years, as I've weeded out the takers and I've surrounded myself with people that are ahead of me and that I'm looking up to, that's only been a positive for me.

John Kavanagh, *The Mike Dolce Show 143*, July 18, 2016

Some people scatter thoughts of fear, doubt, and failure wherever they go. Whenever we're with them, we have no desire to exert ourselves. We can feel that they have no sympathy with our goals, and our instinct is to guard closely any expression of our larger aim in life.

Others stimulate our mental processes and stir us to our depths with a determination to make something of ourselves. It is impossible to associate with ambitious people without catching their spirit to some extent. The atmosphere they create carries grand possibilities and encourages us to think of a better future for ourselves. We are driven by the feeling that we must not disappoint those who believe in us and help us see in ourselves potential that was invisible to us before.

I don't have that many friends. I have a close circle of people that I talk to ... and then that's it—nobody else exists. I'm just tunnel vision on

---

this path, and anyone that tries to come in and steer me away from it ... I just end up getting rid of them.

Conor McGregor, A Day in Dublin, MMAFighting, July 17, 2014

Many people go through their whole lives buried in an atmosphere that stifles hope and aspiration. And they go to their graves with the best in them still dormant. If only these people could have cut themselves off from their negative influences, it may have transformed their whole experience of life.

It is much easier to keep up our interest and enthusiasm when we are around others who are pursuing an ambition and forging ahead despite great difficulties. We must be willing to make any sacrifice necessary to get into an environment that stimulates our self-development. We must keep close only those who understand us and encourage us to make the most of ourselves.

Any time I'd drift off, John would always reel me back in and reinforce the dream. He'd say, "We can do it. Let's do it. This is what you need to do. We need to show up here. We need to put in more hours than everybody. It needs to be every single second of your life. There cannot be no outside." And that's what happened.

Conor McGregor Exclusive, eir Sport, September 10, 2014

SINGLENESS OF PURPOSE

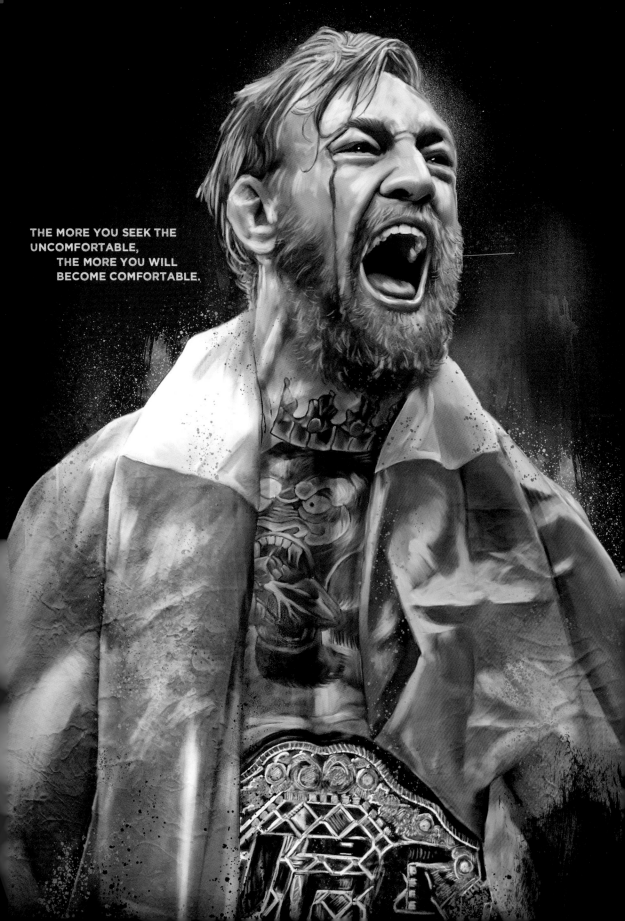

THE MORE YOU SEEK THE
UNCOMFORTABLE,
  THE MORE YOU WILL
BECOME COMFORTABLE.

UFC Fight Night 46.
McGregor versus Brandao.
July 19, 2014. Dublin, Ireland.

The pressure of Conor fighting in front of his hometown.

The pressure of his first UFC main event.

The pressure of his first fight in eleven months, following the worst injury of his career.

In the lead-up to the event, Conor was asked again and again how he was handling the pressure. Days before the fight, MMA journalist Ariel Helwani put the question like this: "Considering you haven't fought in eleven months, are you almost anxious to get back in there? How would you describe your emotions just a couple days away?"

> *Honestly, I am calm, composed, prepared—I have never felt better. Like I said, I feel different. People are saying there's all this pressure. **I want this illusion of pressure 'cause I don't feel jack-shit, Ariel, yeah? I want more of it.***
>
> Conor McGregor Predicts He Will Be Champion, MMAFighting, July 16, 2014

The spirit in which a person faces their adversity—whether they approach it like one destined for victory or like one who has already been defeated—goes a long way in determining the level of success possible for them.

Few people realize they have the power to choose what kind of attitude they bring into any situation—and that the quality of their attitudes affect their experiences and influence the ability they have to overcome challenges. As Conor has shown many times in his career, the mere act of asserting one's ability to conquer opposition gives strength to the faculties which doubt and fear undermine.

In an interview with Tony McGregor, Conor's father, he noted that Conor and his coach practice not only "new moves," but also "new thoughts, new ideas, new mental attitudes." John Kavanagh has not made a secret of the attitude he tries to instill in his fighters:

Conor McGregor Effect, BT Sport, December 9, 2015

> *I try to get my guys to run towards—**run towards**—stress, both physically and mentally. And run towards challenges that they might lose, because that's what will lead to adaptation.*
>
> John Kavanagh, *The Mike Dolce Show 143*, July 18, 2016

The idea that attitudes are critical to success is nothing new, but the mindset Conor was flaunting before his first UFC main event is far beyond what most people have in mind when they use the word. This is not about the attitude of 'I can' versus 'I can't.' Saying to oneself 'I can' is better than saying 'I can't,' but the problem with it is that it still suggests struggle. It still reinforces that the experience is bad. It still signals to the brain that whatever we're telling ourselves we can do is something we don't want to be doing.

Conor is showing a different approach. He is showing us how to actually change the relationship we have with adversity—from one in which we are hoping to endure it, to one in which we are completely comfortable with it.

That is what perfection is about. That is what getting to a high, high level is about—to be comfortable in the uncomfortable.

Conor McGregor, Welcome to my Office, MMAWeekly, September 24, 2014

Allowing our minds to resist an experience that cannot or should not be avoided is an acknowledgment of weakness. It admits of a powerlessness to act as we desire. The powerlessness does not arise from the actual experience, but from our mental relationship with it.

Whenever a person encounters adversity, the attitude they adopt can be their greatest strength or their most crippling weakness. By welcoming his adversity, by saying "I want more of it," Conor

assumes a dominant mentality that instantly shrinks
the power the situation has over him. It is the same
attitude he had towards Dustin Poirier when, four
seconds before landing the shot that ended the
fight, Conor asked him, "What you got, pussy?"

UFC 178, 3:22 of
the first round

Other people cannot make us afraid. They may
do things that scare others, but it is only when we
allow our minds to shrink from their threats that
we experience fear.

The same is true of circumstances. The trials we
face in life only overwhelm us when we concede
that they are more than we can handle. Nothing
can affect us until we give it control through our
own mental resistance. The instant we welcome our
adversity, the power it has over us disappears. That
which strikes terror into one person's heart may not
even cause another to wince.

*Adversity causes some men to break and others to
break records.*

Conor McGregor quoting William Arthur Ward, *The MMA Hour 175*, April 8, 2013

The power to choose one's attitude is immortal,
indestructible—something that cannot be harmed
by outside forces. No matter how overwhelming
an experience seems, we always have the ability
to laugh at the situation, to look down on it, to
assert our superiority. As Viktor Frankl wrote in

Man's Search for Meaning, "Everything can be taken from a man but one thing: the last of the human freedoms—to choose one's attitude in any given set of circumstances."

To some people, the way ahead seems so full of obstacles that they never get anywhere. But those who seek out and welcome experiences that challenge them will soon find they are far stronger than any adversity they encounter.

> *I remember when I first started sparring—when I'd go down to the gym and I knew I was going to spar that day, I'd have these nerves in my stomach. And I used to always celebrate those nerves, because I knew, "These nerves feel the exact same as the nerves that I felt when this kid was trying to fight me." ... So I would always seek that feeling.*
>
> Conor McGregor with Jim Gray, SHOWTIME, August 24, 2017

The attitudes a person chooses are patterns that are constantly weaving themselves into their character. Few people develop the mentality required to ignore the internal voice that urges them to run from opposition. The majority are always consumed by resistance, always dwelling on the difficulty in front of them, always questioning themselves.

CONOR MCGREGOR

Obstacles always shrink or grow according to our attitude towards them. If our minds are filled with resistance, obstacles appear insurmountable. But if we accept and appreciate the trials we encounter, obstacles look tiny compared to what awaits us on the other side. Everything that opposes us loses its substance the moment we begin to grapple with it.

It's important just to still the mind. Calm it. Make everything smaller than it is.

Conor McGregor, UFC 194 Lunch Scrum, MMAFighting, December 2, 2015

Everyone understands in hindsight that the most challenging experiences they go through are the ones that force them to evolve. The most successful individuals are those who see the truth of this so clearly that they pursue every experience that will open up their character. They seek the uncomfortable and view their battles with adversity as opportunities to become stronger *as those battles are happening,* instead of just in retrospect.

Conor wasn't born with a desire to put himself through stressful situations. What propelled him forward was the understanding he gained at a young age that the more a person draws on their courage, the more courage they will have. His recognition of this was the driving force of his entire career.

---

*Ultimately that is what drove me to combat sports ... to be able to be comfortable in an uncomfortable situation. So every time I would go to a boxing gym, I would feel those butterflies that I felt that time, and I'd be thinking, "Yes, now I'm getting more comfortable. Now I'm feeling these feelings more—the more I feel them, the more I'm gonna become comfortable in them." So I would always search for that feeling. Eventually it moved on from just walking in through the gym doors having those butterflies—now it's time to spar. Sparring I'd get even more butterflies, and I'd be just trying to grow and grow and grow. Then it's competition, now let's compete—now I'm getting crazy butterflies. And eventually you just become comfortable with it—**now I'm fuckin' fighting at the MGM Grand and I don't give a shit.***

Conor McGregor, Welcome to my Office, MMAWeekly, September 24, 2014

Strength of character is something that must be earned from conquered obstacles. By following the process Conor describes above, we can train our minds to become comfortable in nearly any situation. The effects of cultivating such a mind can be seen every time Conor fights. His confidence and comfort tower over his opponents at every

———————

stage—during the interviews and press conferences, the weigh-ins and stare-downs, and the fights themselves.

Most people take for granted that they use all the ability they possess, but unless a person has learned the habit of throwing themselves head-first into the things that will force their evolution, they can never know what they are capable of. No ordinary effort will bring out anyone's best. No half-hearted exertion will lead to any remarkable self-discoveries.

> *You could see me [bouncing around] backstage before that Dublin card. I honestly was walking out [thinking], "Is this supposed to be pressure? Is this supposed to be the moment where people choke?" I felt like this was easy. These are the feelings that I've been feeling my whole life. These are the feelings that I've been chasing my whole life.*
>
> Conor McGregor, Welcome to my Office, MMAWeekly, September 24, 2014

The cause of the great unrest that many people feel is an inward call for the undiscovered part of themselves. It is only those who have stopped growing that are satisfied with their achievements. Anyone who is still evolving can sense their own lack of fulfillment. They are always dissatisfied

———————

with what they have done, always reaching out for something larger and more complete.

Satisfaction is an emotion for the middle, for the people left in the mid-tier. So I don't get satisfied.

Conor McGregor, UFC Fight Night Boston Backstage, January 19, 2015

After welcoming the pressure that came with the fight in Dublin, Conor could not have scripted a more perfect night. Not only did he knock out Diego Brandao in the first round—as he had predicted—but all four fighters from Conor's gym were victorious, making it a proud and dominant night for Ireland. In the months that followed the event, Conor's lingering hunger and lack of satisfaction foreshadowed that it was just the first of many successes.

*Everything was just perfect. ... I set out to bring [the UFC back to Ireland], I set out to help my teammates ... I said I was gonna do it and then I went out and done it. **But with that, it's done. I'm over it now.** I'm not gonna stare at it. You stare at your past, and you'll end up staying there. It's OK to look back and admire it, but you carry on. I'm not in the business of staring back at it. You know what I mean? And getting lost back there. People say a loss can make or break a fighter, but trust me, a win can also make or*

---

break a fighter, because they get comfortable with a win. People can get comfortable with a win and slack off then—slack off on the training, slack off on the diet. They've won one. They're winners now. That's not me, you know. You sleep on a win and you'll wake up with a loss. So I just carry on. ... I'm not stopping here. Trust me when I tell you this—I am only warming up. You can get used to this face.

Conor McGregor Exclusive, eir Sport, September 10, 2014

Singleness of Purpose

―――――――――

THE DAY YOU STOP TRYING TO LEARN
IS THE DAY YOU'RE GETTING READY TO LOSE.

A fter knocking out Dustin Poirier in a tidy 106 seconds—a performance he would later describe using the phrase "preparation meets opportunity"—Conor McGregor donned his Louis Vuitton aviator sunglasses, buttoned up his ivory suit, and sat down at the UFC 178 post-fight press conference to answer questions. Midway through, the following question was asked: "Conor, we hear guys all the time say they're getting better with every fight, but it really seems true with you. What's been the key to that? What have you figured out that's making you have a better performance every time?"

Conor began with what sounded like a typical answer, outlining the amount of training he puts himself through to perform at his best.

I just put the work in. I don't slack off. Three hundred and sixty-five days a year, twenty-four-seven, I am getting better. That's what it's about. This game is about growth.

At this point, where most athletes would have cut their answer short, Conor made another point, highlighting the *quality* of his training by pointing out the unsophisticated approach taken by some of his fellow fighters.

I find that a lot of mixed martial artists—or a lot of athletes period—get to a stage where they are happy with their ability, and then it's about maintenance. It's about showing up at the gym, it's about getting hard rounds in, it's about getting miles on the road in, but really their skill level is not growing.

Conor McGregor, UFC 178 Post-Fight Press Conference, September 27, 2014

Conor is often told that he's the best trash-talker in sports. His response to this label is that he doesn't talk trash, he talks truth. His words above are a perfect example of that distinction. The routine Conor is identifying—of undergoing hours of training with a focus on working hard rather than on learning—is well-known to those who study human performance and the acquisition of mastery. In the science of expertise it goes by the name 'naive practice.'

Naive practice is a term coined by Anders Ericsson, an eminent psychologist based out of Florida State University. In his highly-acclaimed book *Peak: Secrets from the New Science of Expertise* (2016), Ericsson identifies the principles that help a person avoid naive practice and work towards elite performance using what is called 'purposeful practice.'

Whereas Conor echoes Ericsson's work most often by describing and condemning naive practice, his coach refers to it more directly. In an interview on *The Mike Dolce Show*, John Kavanagh summarized his approach to teaching new techniques by saying, "I'm big about purposeful practice."

The concepts of naive and purposeful practice can be applied to any domain of human expertise. Whatever we do, if we want to work our way towards mastery, we need to engage in purposeful practice. So what exactly do the two terms mean?

NAIVE PRACTICE

We are engaging in naive practice whenever we expect to continually advance our level of skill by simply doing an activity. If the activity is playing an instrument, naive practice is getting through a song. If the activity is chess, naive practice is playing through a game. And, as Conor describes, if the activity is martial arts, naive practice is fighting or sparring.

A lot of people get to a stage where they think, "Okay, I just show up, and I just spar, and I just run, and I just roll," but they're not trying to learn.

CONOR MCGREGOR

That was a thing I realized over in Iceland. Rather than just showing up and going "hell-for-leather," I was slowing it down and just really trying to learn everything and pick up off everything, and I feel my game has elevated, definitely.

Conor McGregor, SevereMMA, December 24, 2012

Most people gravitate towards naive practice because it is easier and because they don't know any better. They don't know any better because whenever anyone is an absolute beginner at something, they will see a certain amount of improvement by simply engaging in the activity. When everything is brand new, even the least focused and motivated among us will make adaptations and notice ourselves improving.

The biggest limitation of naive practice is discovered at the inevitable 'plateau'—the point at which mindlessly doing an activity only helps us to maintain our current skill level, rather than leading to further advancement. Unless we hear someone like Conor illuminating the pitfalls of naive practice, we often don't realize that we've shifted into autopilot and stopped improving.

So many martial artists get into a situation where they stay the same. They get to a level, and then it's maintain. It's about maintenance—bring guys

[90]

———————

in, spar hard, stay fit, but you're not growing to that next level, you're not experimenting with new shots. ... And again, I'm only scratching the surface on all this. I only feel like I'm learning all this myself, and that's why I believe I'm a step ahead of these people.

Conor McGregor, Welcome to my Office, MMAWeekly, September 24, 2014

Note that when Conor spoke these words, he was already proclaiming himself to be the best fighter in his division, yet he was still speaking as if he had a never-ending supply of new things to learn. This mindset—of having absolute confidence in one's ability to keep getting better—is central to purposeful practice. When our practice methods are correct, we see that we can improve whatever facet of our craft we focus our attention on. We understand that there need not be an end to this process—that with the correct approach, we can always make refinements in whatever area we choose.

PURPOSEFUL PRACTICE
So, what are some of the training principles that have helped Conor dominate the fight game? What has science proven to be most effective in developing mastery? And what things do many of the

———————

best coaches, trainers, and performers in the world incorporate into their practice?

1.   Set specific, well-defined goals

For any practice session, we need to know exactly which aspect of our craft we're trying to improve. The key to learning anything new is to break it down into smaller components. Once we have established the pieces of a skill, we should find or design activities that target those pieces individually, and set increasingly challenging goals for ourselves as we perform them. Once we are comfortable with each piece, we can slowly integrate them into the bigger picture.

2.   Focus intensely

The more intensely we focus while practicing a skill, the faster our brain will make adaptations, significantly speeding up the learning process. Watching Conor hit pads, it is clear that he maintains the same intensity in training as he does when he's in a fight. Focusing is not easy—it is a skill we must develop alongside everything else. Anyone who is unable to focus intensely will have their potential severely limited.

3.   Get instructive feedback

Any time we try to do something, we get the basic feedback of whether we have succeeded or failed, but this does not necessarily help us improve. Instructive feedback tells us *why* we have failed and *how* we can change our approach to get better. Take chess as an example. The feedback we get from playing a game of chess (naive practice) is whether we win or lose. Better feedback would be a computer chess program pointing out our bad moves and suggesting superior alternatives. The best feedback would be an expert explaining how the thought process that led to our bad moves was flawed or incomplete.

4.   Operate outside our comfort zone

Whenever we do anything new or beyond our abilities, we experience discomfort. Many people recoil from this feeling, but it is always the activities that make us uncomfortable that lead to the greatest improvement. The goals we set for each of our practice activities should always be just beyond what we can perform comfortably. Once the feeling of discomfort disappears, our progress will halt.

THE BEGINNER'S MINDSET

There is a tendency for people who have reached a certain level of ability in their craft to get accustomed to the feeling of competence and then relax their approach to training. They become

---

satisfied with their performance and fall into the trap of naive practice because it is more enjoyable than going through the discomfort required to get to the next level.

As a way of rejecting this tendency, Conor always approaches his training with a beginner's mindset. He always sees himself as having an unlimited number of things left to learn, and this humility is part of what allows him to continue to reach higher levels of mastery.

> *I am number one in my craft, in my game. But I still show up every day as a white-belt. I show up every day as a day-one beginner.*
>
> Conor McGregor *Unfiltered*, Sports Illustrated, February 24, 2016

Maintaining a beginner's mindset is difficult because much of the work we do to expand our skills is to relieve the discomfort we experience as beginners. The game-changer is in recognizing that this feeling of discomfort is what forces the brain to adapt. If we are committed to becoming the best we can be, we need to make sure we are constantly challenging ourselves.

> *If you ever get to a stage where you're looking at something and saying, "Na, that doesn't work. My way is better," that's the wrong way of thinking. You wanna learn absolutely everything. You*

_____

wanna absorb everything. You wanna be perfect, you know, you're looking for perfection.

Conor McGregor, SevereMMA, December 24, 2012

APPLYING PURPOSEFUL PRACTICE

As a mixed martial arts coach with a large gym and a long list of professional fighters under his banner, John Kavanagh has had endless opportunities to experiment with what works to upgrade the skills of his students. In a discussion about his training, he described the approach he takes using the concept of a closed loop.

> *I'm big into closed loops. I don't see the point in just practicing. We need to practice, we need to go back and see what was wrong with that practice, and we need to improve in the next session. And if you keep that closed loop going for long enough, you have to get better. And provably so—it's not a theory, it's not my opinion. That's a fact. You read about anybody who's great at what they do, and they all have closed loops. They all go back on themselves and see, "Where were the errors, how can I improve?"*

John Kavanagh, *The Mike Dolce Show 143*, July 18, 2016

A closed loop is a process that makes refinements through repetition. A step-by-step closed loop

_____

involving the principles of purposeful practice might look something like this:

1. Identify a weakness in your domain of expertise.
2. Form a clear mental picture of what it would look and feel like to gain the skill that would fill in that weakness.
3. Break the new skill down into its most basic components.
4. Find or design activities that target those components.
5. Perform those activities with intense focus.
6. Use various forms of feedback to refine and repeat Steps 2 to 5 (especially Step 5) until each component can be reliably performed.
7. Carefully integrate each component until they feel natural and will not be forgotten.

The most effective way to move through each of these steps depends on what activity we're learning. The Brazilian Jiu-Jitsu classes at Conor's gym and most other BJJ schools follow the above progression exactly:

1. The instructor chooses a skill.
2. The instructor demonstrates the skill to give the students a clear mental picture of it.
3. The instructor breaks the skill down into its individual movements.

4. Students pair up to practice the skill one movement at a time.
5. Students try to perform each movement correctly, and then slowly combine them and increase the speed.
6. Feedback is given by partners and instructors as the skill is repeated.
7. Students spar in a way designed to incorporate the new skill.

As in this example, the guidance of an expert is often helpful to move through these steps efficiently. Competing at a world-class level in any highly-developed discipline generally requires outside instruction.

However, no matter what our goals, and whether or not we have the benefit of an instructor, going through the process of researching and thinking thoroughly about how we can improve is critical. John remembers Conor doing this kind of work very early on.

What made [Conor] a little bit different was I could see right from the beginning he was very curious about how Jiu-Jitsu worked and how martial arts worked. Whereas some guys might come in and train hard when they're in the gym, but then they kind of switch-off and go home and

---

do other stuff. I could see Conor was, pretty early on, fairly obsessive. He would be always thinking about it outside of training ... and he was always questioning what I would show him, and maybe come up with his own way of doing things. As a coach I've noticed over the years that the guys who tend to get better quicker are the ones who are thinking about it a lot more.

John Kavanagh, *The Rise of Conor McGregor*, MTV UK, March 7, 2013

SINGLENESS OF PURPOSE

THERE'S NO TALENT HERE.
THIS IS HARD WORK.
THIS IS AN OBSESSION.
TALENT DOES NOT EXIST.

When Conor McGregor first walked through the doors of Crumlin Boxing Club, tracking a line of small, muddy footprints straight to the heavy bags, he had some advantages over other kids just starting out. His advantages were not the qualities that make the difference in fighting—speed, technique, and the ability to read one's opponent—those would only come after years of training. His advantages were the qualities that make the difference in every domain of human expertise, the qualities immediately accessible to all of us—enthusiasm, self-belief, and the willingness to work hard.

Report of this comes from Phil Sutcliffe, two-time boxing Olympian, owner of the gym, and one of the key figures that helped Conor develop his striking skills through his early teenage years: "[Conor] was like any other novice who we taught the basics to." "He was a good kid, did what he was told. He wasn't particularly special in the boxing, but he did try hard. And once anyone tries hard, you can make them special."

Conor has called himself many things—*the hardest*

Quotes from skysports.com and *Conor McGregor Effect* Documentary *worker in the game, the 170-pound Irish gorilla,* and way back in 2008, seconds after knocking out his opponent in his fourth professional fight, *the fucking future.* But there's one word you'll never hear Conor or his coach use to describe him, and that word is talented.

> *The amount of times I'm told what an incredible natural talent Conor is, and [told], "If he wasn't such a natural athlete, he wouldn't have got as far as he did," and to be honest I find that it's insulting towards him. I've seen the work rate. I've seen him be the first one in here and be the last one out— me having to forcibly kick him out of the gym. He's done that for over ten years, and now people are seeing the fruits of that labor, and they call it natural talent. I can do nothing but smile at that.*
>
> John Kavanagh, *Conor McGregor Effect,* BT Sport, December 9, 2015

People have very strong and vastly different beliefs about talent, and it's a problem. It's a problem because talent—or lack of talent—is used around the world as an excuse not to try, not to bother exerting oneself.

However, a growing number are speaking out rejecting that talent exists. This group includes many who have dominated their fields—from people like Michelangelo and Albert Einstein, to

Wayne Gretzky and Jack Nicklaus. Each of these experts have resisted the idea that their success came from any inborn ability, instead attributing it to the unwavering devotion they gave to their disciplines.

While most rookies and amateurs are happy to be called talented, some of the world's highest achievers are actually offended by the label. Take Ray Allen for example. In an interview with ESPN shortly before he broke the record for the most three-pointers in NBA history, he said, "I've argued this with a lot of people in my life. When people say God blessed me with a beautiful jump shot, it really pisses me off. I tell those people, 'Don't undermine the work I've put in every day.' Not some days. Every day. Ask anyone who has been on a team with me who shoots the most. Go back to Seattle and Milwaukee and ask them. The answer is me."

People who dedicate their lives to the pursuit of excellence usually learn something along the way that many others never do. They learn that what separates the masterful from the mediocre is not talent—it's the right training over a long enough period of time.

I don't believe in talent. Talent doesn't exist.

*I believe in working harder and putting in the time—being completely obsessed. And, yeah, I think that's life. I mean, [I knocked out Jose Aldo in 13 seconds], but it was an entire lifetime of work to get to that 13 seconds. **It's not about what's obvious. It's about all that's not obvious that goes into success.***

Conor McGregor on training, TheMacLife, October 18, 2016

Recently, the notion of natural talent has also been opposed by psychologists who study human performance. In his book *Peak*, Anders Ericsson summarized the scientific consensus on the concept of talent in the following way: "By now it is safe to conclude from many studies on a wide variety of disciplines that nobody develops extraordinary abilities without putting in tremendous amounts of practice. I do not know of any serious scientist who doubts that conclusion."

This is exactly what Conor and his coach mean when they say talent doesn't exist. Talent is defined as "the natural ability to do something well," and no one is born with the natural ability to do something well. What is called exceptional talent is always the result of some exceptional period of learning, unseen by those who only see the effects of that learning.

―――――――――

If someone walks in and is what we would say "athletically gifted," well, he didn't play video games for the last ten years, and then walk in and be able to have a good vertical jump or be able to walk on a balance beam. ... He probably climbed a lot of trees, he probably ran around the area with his friends, he probably played some different sports. And if you have all that, then someone walks in and they can kind of move in a certain way.

John Kavanagh, *The Mike Dolce Show 143*, July 18, 2016

Some see the effects of hard work and immediately attribute them to natural ability. They have no knowledge of what led to such ability, of the massive effort put forth. They do not see the trials and failures that people with great skill have endured to gain their expertise. And it is only their ignorance of the work behind the mastery that enables them to credit it to talent.

Conor was inspired for whatever reason a bunch of years ago to pursue this dream, and he killed himself in the gym, every day. That's what I saw for the last ten years. Now people look at him fighting and go, "Oh, he's so talented."

John Kavanagh, *The MMA Hour 290*, July 15, 2015

We often hear people saying they would do

―――――――――

this or that if they only had the ability—if they were only talented enough. And they justify their mediocre lives by claiming that they lack the gifts given to others. These people do not use a trace of the potential they have. Wherever someone is lamenting their lack of talent and using it to excuse themselves from ambition, there is always someone close by who has succeeded under worse starting conditions and made their mark on the world.

GENETIC ADVANTAGES

Although no one is born with the natural ability to do something well, there is no denying that genetic variance can play a part in determining a person's potential for an activity. It is hard to imagine someone who is naturally very thin playing as a linebacker in the NFL, whereas such a person may have a considerable advantage as a long-distance runner or rock climber.

However, for every career that a person's genetic makeup might close them off to, the doors to a hundred other careers stand wide open. With the correct training methods and sufficient determination, almost anyone can excel in whatever domain they dedicate themselves to.

The main reason for this is that, even at the highest levels of any discipline, very few people sustain a lifestyle that will ever bring them close to their maximum potential. That is why those with the best genes are not always at the top. If we imagined a world in which everyone led a life perfectly designed to make them the best they could be at a certain activity, then only genetic advantages would determine who became elite. But because we live in a world in which almost no one realizes their full potential, differences in genetics can be overcome by differences in dedication and effort.

One of the worst things that can happen to a person in terms of realizing their potential is for them to believe they were born without talent and are thus limited in what they can achieve. This conviction colors their whole attitude towards life and is responsible for innumerable failures. We should all see ourselves in a much grander light, should think of ourselves as having unlimited possibilities. Rather than focusing on anything we lack, we should focus on what we each possess—a brain that can acquire any skill it devotes its attention to.

The word talent makes my eye twitch. I really hate that word. It's kind of like saying there's something

---

---

magical happening. I don't believe in magic, and I don't believe in talent.

John Kavanagh, *The MMA Hour 290*, July 15, 2015

What [Conor] did have was an aptitude towards training. When he's in the gym, you can't get him out of it. ... He was obsessive about it. He was gonna do nothing else all day, every day other than train. That quality leads to someone being many years later described as talented, but really it's not, really he had the only quality that mattered, and that was that he loved it. And he kept coming, he kept showing up.

John Kavanagh, *Conor McGregor Effect*, BT Sport, December 9, 2015

People who succeed do not make excuses, they work. They do not whine, they keep forging ahead. They do not wait for someone to help them, they help themselves. Those who complain of insufficient natural ability confess the weakness of their will and show that they are not equal to the opportunities surrounding them.

The force that carries us forward is not our talent. It is our energy, our determination, our originality. Every individual would be amazed if they could see unfolded in front of them all the potential they have—if they could only catch a glimpse of the many people they might become.

You could be anyone. *If you put in the time, you will reach the top and that is that. I am not talented. I am obsessed.*

Conor McGregor, *SC Featured: Notorious*, ESPN, December 9, 2015

ALL THAT MATTERS
IS HOW YOU SEE
YOURSELF.

C onor McGregor started living out his dreams on April 6, 2013.

After running through Marcus Brimage in his sixty-seven-second debut, Conor met with UFC president Dana White backstage, was given a spot on the post-fight press conference, and was handed his first paychecks—$8,000 to show, $8,000 to win, and a $60,000 knockout-of-the-night bonus. Weeks later, Conor gave a short interview during which he was asked, "What do you wanna be?"

With everything he had been working for coming to fruition, it would have been natural to expect Conor to reiterate the aspirations he had laid out in the past—*a UFC champion, a self-made millionaire, a national hero*. Instead, this was his reply:

> *There's another thing—"What do you wanna be?" I don't wanna be anything. I am everything I wanna be. I'm already there. ... People say "I want this," or "I wanna do this and I wanna do that," but **if the vibe you're putting out is want, you're always gonna want.** I always have the*

Conor said that his least favorite word is "want" during an interview with CNN, November 14, 2016

---

attitude that I have. ... I don't want anything. I have everything. That's the mindset I'm in.

Conor McGregor, Shinobi Vlog, July 5, 2013

For all his dedication to future achievement, all the intensity of his ambition, one mistake Conor never made was thinking he had to wait until he achieved everything he was working towards in order to be happy. He realized very early that by assuming his situation is one of abundance and opportunity, he could help create the conditions that would attract those things into his life.

You've gotta feel like it's already there. You've gotta feel like you're living it already. And then carry on with your work and just carry on doing what you do—focusing on what you love, chasing your dream, and believing in your ability. And nothing can stop you then, absolutely nothing.

Conor McGregor, Ireland AM on TV3, July 15, 2014

Most people spend a large portion of their life stuck in anticipation of the future. They are never living the life they are working to achieve, but just getting ready to live—just hoping to be happy sometime in the future. They don't realize that what they are searching for either lives in themselves or nowhere, that if they do not take happiness with

---

———

them as a principle, they may search the world over without ever finding it.

In another interview that came shortly after Conor notched his first UFC win, he was asked, "What's your grand plan now—what do you wanna do?" Conor seemed almost offended at the thought that his plans would be altered.

> *Nothing changes for me. I already felt like I had money back then even though I didn't have money. I always felt like I was the champ even though I wasn't the champ. Nothing changes for me.*
>
> Conor McGregor, *The Late Late Show*, RTÉ, April 13, 2013

Every person ought to play the part of their ambition, ought to assume in each moment that they are already what they intend to be. It is no different from what a great actor does. They see themselves as and feel that they actually are the character they are impersonating. They live the part they are playing on stage, whether it be that of a hero or a beggar. If they are playing a hero, they think like a hero and talk like a hero. Everything about them radiates heroism. And if the part they take is that of a beggar, they dress like one and carry themselves like one.

> *Act and you will become.*
>
> Conor McGregor after Cage Warriors 55, SevereMMA, June 1, 2013

———

If we wish to attain success, we must take on the role of a successful person. We must live every moment of our lives as the hero of our own story. Few things are as important in a person's life as the kind of part they see themselves playing. Whether they think it is small and tragic, or grand and noble, their life will correspond.

There is a great difference between a person who goes about the world like a conqueror and one who always acts as if they have been defeated in life. Everything a person encounters in the world is shaped by their mentality. The perception of always seeing ourselves as fortunate—of feeling grateful just for being alive—will put our minds in a creative, producing state.

> *Gratitude is one of the strongest forms of power in attracting good things. ... I always felt grateful for even the small things. ... I always celebrated every little good thing that would happen in my life, even before I had any kind of money or any of that. I would celebrate and I would feel grateful for that, and it gave me more.*

Conor McGregor, UFC Has Struck Gold, MMAFighting, May 29, 2015

There is something in the attitude of every person that offers a prediction of their future. The way they speak and carry themselves, the energy and initiative they put into their work—each of these is an indication of what is awaiting them.

Excellence is not a skill. Excellence is an attitude.

Conor McGregor quoting Ralph Marston, The MMA Hour 175, April 8, 2013

It is impossible to hide the quality of our thoughts from others for long. We cannot help but broadcast through our words and mannerisms what the substance of our minds is worth. The atmosphere we bring around with us is contagious and will quickly be perceived by those we come into contact with.

[Conor's] just such a positive guy. You always feel good when you're around him. He makes people feel good. I think that's what people appreciate about him. You watch an interview with Conor, and you come away feeling good, and I think that's why people are attracted to him as a person. And that's why I love being around him. I always feel a positive energy around him.

Cathal Pendred, Conor McGregor Effect, BT Sport, December 9, 2015

Many people grow up in conditions that keep them ignorant of their possibilities. But once a person has proven beyond question that they have potential that has never been called forth, it is nearly impossible they will ever again be satisfied with a return to their former lives.

I love this life. It's important for me to remind

---

myself that I love it. There's definitely days where I'm like, "Fuck all of this. I'm out of here." ... But, I remind myself why I do it, what I do it for. And then I just re-energize myself to it. This is the life I have chosen. This is the life I have built. This life is not for everyone. It's for the insanely driven individual. And that's what I feel I am. I am insane to this game.

Conor McGregor, UFC 194 LA Scrum, MMAFighting, September 2, 2015

The mind is made for work, and when it is idle all sorts of troubles begin. Nothing can give a person a greater sense of wellbeing than working every day in the pursuit of a worthy purpose. Much of the enjoyment in life does not come from actual achievement but from the anticipation of what we feel we can accomplish. The perception that we are growing and advancing gives a perpetual satisfaction that nothing else can offer.

It cannot be emphasized too strongly that what each of us will amount to in this world depends absolutely on the way we spend our time. It is our time—the days, hours, and minutes of our lives—that we must use to get what we want out of life. All the success that will ever be ours must come through the correct use of the instant we are passing through. We ought to live each second as

---

---

if our whole existence was telescoped down to the single day ahead of us.

We all have the same 24 hours of the day.

Conor McGregor, *The MMA Hour 211*, December 9, 2013

In each moment of a person's life, they are a slave or a master. As they surrender to temptation, as they bow in defeat to any condition, to any environment, to any failure, they are a slave. But as they crush out human weakness, defeat opposing elements within themselves, and create a new self out of their former existence, they are a master.

With no idle regret for the past, no useless worry for the future, we should live each day as if it were the only day left to assert all that is best in us, the only day left to conquer all that is worst in us. We should strive to overcome the weak elements within at every slight manifestation. Each day, then, must be a victory for us.

At the end of the day, you've gotta feel some way. So why not feel unbeatable? Why not feel untouchable? Why not feel like the best to ever do it?

Conor McGregor, Ireland AM on TV3, July 15, 2014

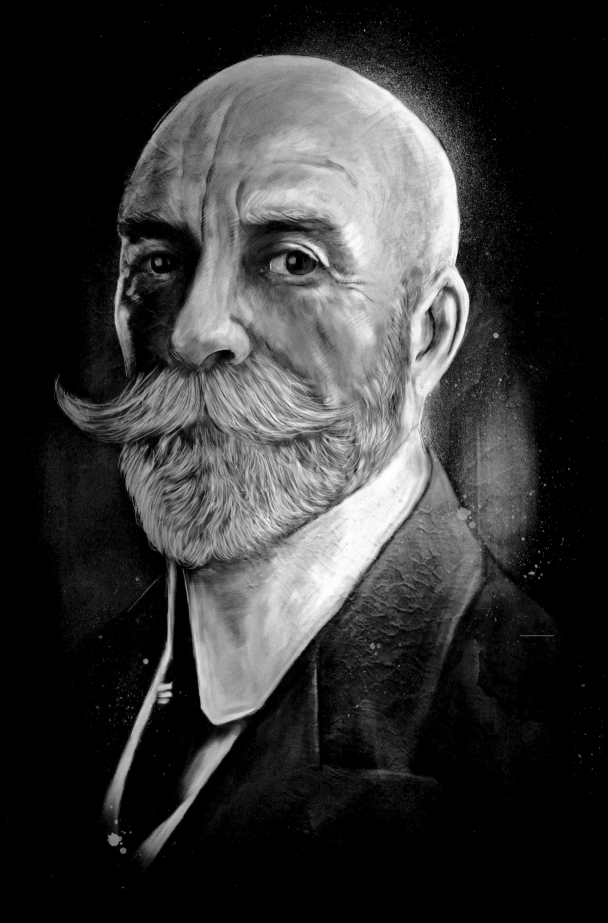

In addition to Conor McGregor, this book was greatly inspired by the work of American writer Orison Swett Marden (1848-1924). *One hundred and fifty pounds of human flesh and blood weigh nothing on the scale of manhood without weight of will and tenacity of purpose.*

Orison Swett Marden, *The Making of a Man*, 1905

For questions, comments, or to receive a document with links to video of the quotes used in this book, email singlenessofpurposebook@gmail.com

APPENDIX

Cover art done from photograph by Ramsey Cardy via Sportsfile.

Page 4: Art done from photograph by Josh Hedges/ Zuffa LLC via Getty Images. Quote by Conor McGregor from *Notorious* TV series, RTÉ, January 26, 2015.

Page 8: Art done from photograph by Rosie Cohe/ SHOWTIME via Sportsfile. Quote by Conor McGregor from *The Rise of Conor McGregor* documentary, MTV UK, March 7, 2013.

Page 22: Art done from photograph by Ramsey Cardy via Sportsfile. Quote by Conor McGregor from *Notorious* documentary, RTÉ, March 13, 2014.

Page 36: Art done from photograph by Esther Lin via Sportsfile. Quote by Conor McGregor from *An Experience with Conor McGregor* Manchester interview, January 28, 2017.

Page 52: Art done from photograph by Mark J. Rebilas via Sportsfile. Quote by Conor McGregor from Twitter, February 5, 2014.

Page 64: Art done from photograph by Ramsey Cardy via Sportsfile. Quote by Conor McGregor from UFC 189 World Tour LA Media Scrum, MMAFighting, March 24, 2015.

Page 74: Art done from photograph by Esther Lin via Sportsfile. Quote by Conor McGregor from *Conor McGregor Unfiltered*, Sports Illustrated, February 24, 2016.

Page 86: Art done from photograph by Ramsey Cardy via Sportsfile. Quote by Conor McGregor from SevereMMA interview, December 24, 2012.

Page 100: Art done from photograph by Josh Dahl via Sportsfile. Quote by Conor McGregor from *SC Featured: Notorious*, ESPN, December 9, 2015.

Page 110: Art done from photograph by Josh Hedges/Zuffa LLC via Getty Images. Quote by Conor McGregor from *The Rise of Conor McGregor documentary*, MTV UK, March 7, 2013.